THE MAKING OF

Fight the Future

Also published by HarperPrism

The X-Files: Fight the Future
The X-Files Scrapbook

ATTENTION: ORGANIZATIONS AND CORPORATIONS

Most HarperPrism books are available at special quantity discounts for bulk purchases for sales promotions, premiums, or fund-raising. For information please call or write: Special Markets Department, HarperCollins Publishers, Inc., 10 East 53rd Street, New York, NY 10022–5299. Telephone: (212) 207–7528. Fax: (212) 207–7222.

THE MAKING OF

THE X FILES™

Fight the Future

CREATED BY CHRIS CARTER

Adapted for Young Readers by
JODY DUNCAN

HarperPrism
A Division of HarperCollins*Publishers*

 HarperPrism

A *Division of* HarperCollins*Publishers*
10 East 53rd Street, New York, NY 10022-5299

ISBN 0-06-107316-4

First printing: July 1998

Designed by Laura Lindgren

Printed in the United States of America

Visit HarperPrism on the World Wide Web at http://www.harperprism.com

❖ 10 9 8 7 6 5 4 3 2 1

CONTENTS

1

A PLAGUE AND A PROJECT
(THE STORY)

The X-Files movie begins a long, long time ago, in 35,000 B.C., when much of the earth was covered in ice and snow. Two figures, primitive men, walk through the cold, windswept landscape. They are following the trail left by a mysterious creature. Three-toed tracks lead the hunters to the inside of an ice cave.

The creature is an alien—tall and thin, black-eyed and hairless, with only tiny slits for a nose and mouth. But the alien has razor-sharp teeth and long claws on his hands and feet that extend when it attacks. Suddenly the alien lashes out and fiercely attacks one of the men. One dies in the battle. The second primitive struggles and finally kills the alien. But then we see a scary black oil ooze out of the dead alien's body. It seeps into cracks on the floor and wall. The black oil seems to be alive! It creeps slowly toward the surviving primitive's chest, mouth, and eyes.

1

Without warning, a boy plunges through the roof of the cave. The movie has cut to the present, to Blackwood, Texas, an area outside of Dallas. A group of boys have been playing at the same cave we saw in the first scene. But now,

Stevie (Lucas Black) falls into a cave where his body is invaded by a black, oily fluid—the alien virus.

thirty-five thousand years later, the ice and snow have melted away. Instead, the cave is rocky, and in the middle of empty desert land. The boys, trying to build a fort, have dug a hole in the hard desert ground right above the cave. One of the boys—Stevie (Lucas Black)—digs too deep and suddenly falls through a hole in the earth. He falls so hard the wind is knocked out of him, but he is okay. Exploring the cave, Stevie discovers a human skull and excitedly tells his friends there are lots of bones in the cave. Suddenly, from a crack in the cave floor comes the same gooey, black substance that seeped into the floor thirty-five thousand years earlier. The black oil slowly inches toward the boy. It creeps onto his shoe, crawls under his skin, and moves through his body until even his eyes turn black and oily. Terrified by what has just happened to their friend, the boys run for help. Stevie stands frozen within the cave. The creeping alien oil has paralyzed him.

Suddenly the air is filled with sirens. Soon, there are fire trucks everywhere. Two firemen quickly climb down into the cave to rescue Stevie. Mysteriously, they don't come back. Two more firemen are sent in—and disappear, too. The bodies of all four men have been invaded and infected by the alien oil. The local fire captain is concerned when no one returns from the cave. Now the fire department has to rescue five people instead of one.

Just then, a helicopter swoops down for a landing. Dr. Ben Bronschweig (Jeffrey DeMunn) gets out. He has brought along a mysterious "hazardous materials" team. The team has seen dangerous substances like the black oil

3

The Haz-Mat team led by Dr. Ben
Bronschweig takes over the scene at the cave site.

before. They carefully and quickly carry Stevie's paralyzed body away. The rest of his team begin setting up tents and other equipment at the site. What the local firefighters do not know is that Dr. Bronschweig reports to a secret organization known as "the syndicate." This cave has become an important part of the undercover "project" the syndicate is working on. Dr. Bronschweig will set up a laboratory here to observe one of the infected firemen.

The movie action cuts to a government building one week later. Someone has planted a bomb here. FBI agents must hurry to find the bomb before it goes off. The FBI has cleared out all of the people who work there, and is now looking for where the bomb is hidden.

But two agents have decided to check the building across the street instead. One of them, Fox Mulder (David Duchovny), a handsome man with sad eyes and a quick sense of humor, has a hunch that the FBI is on the wrong track. His longtime partner, Dana Scully (Gillian

TOP/BOTTOM: Mulder and Scully speak to each other by cell phone in the federal building. Mulder is trapped in the vending machine room with the bomb. He needs Scully's help to get everyone—including him—out of the building right away.

5

Anderson), a beautiful red-haired woman, is on the roof of the building, but she speaks to him by cell phone. Together they used to be in charge of the FBI's X-Files unit. But now, that unit has been closed. In the X-Files unit they investigated, or looked into, events that were strange or difficult to explain. Now they are assigned to more common FBI duties—like checking out bomb threats.

Mulder's hunch is right. By accident, he discovers the bomb hidden in a soda machine in the building across

Mulder, Scully, and Special Agent-in-Charge Darius Michaud (Terry O'Quinn) inspect a bomb discovered within a vending machine in the federal building lobby.

the street. With Mulder locked in the vending room, Scully hurries to clear the building. She calls for help from the FBI agents next door. With just minutes to spare, Mulder is rescued by Scully and Special Agent in Charge Darius Michaud (Terry O'Quinn). Michaud orders Mulder and Scully and everyone else out of the building while he stays behind to try to defuse the bomb. As the car speeds away, the bomb goes off. The building explodes in a shower of cement, metal, and broken glass.

A bomb explodes in a Dallas building.

Mulder and Dr. Kurtzweil meet secretly to discuss government conspiracies.

The next day Mulder and Scully are at FBI head-quarters in Washington, D.C., where they are questioned by Assistant Director Jana Cassidy (Blythe Danner). She wants to know everything they saw and heard before the bombing in Dallas. The agents learn that five people were killed in the explosion. Special Agent in Charge Michaud, three firemen, and the young boy, Stevie, all died in the blast. Mulder and Scully also learn that they are being blamed for those deaths.

That night, Mulder meets Dr. Alvin Kurtzweil (Martin Landau). The doctor claims to be an old friend of Mulder's father. He also writes books about government conspiracies—plots to hide information or evidence from the public. Kurtzweil gives Mulder important news. The building in Dallas was bombed by the syndicate to hide the already dead bodies of Stevie and the three firemen. The syndicate did not want anyone to find the bodies, so they blew up the building. Kurtzweil also tells Mulder that Special Agent in Charge Michaud let the building explode because he worked for the syndicate.

Mulder is disturbed by what Kurtzweil has told him. He talks Scully into going to the naval hospital where

Scully infiltrates a hospital morgue to examine the remains of one of the bombing victims. In order to avoid discovery by the military police, she hides in the morgue freezer. When Mulder calls her on the cell phone, the ringing almost gives her away.

the bodies are being kept. At the hospital, they go straight to the cold, dark morgue—a place where dead bodies are temporarily stored. Since Scully was trained as a doctor, she carefully examines the body of one of the bombing victims. She snaps on her medical gloves and does an autopsy—or exam—on one of the firemen. Scully quickly discovers the fireman did not die from the explosion, as someone wanted the agents to believe. He died from some kind of infection. It is one she has never seen before. The victim's skin is almost

Dr. Kurtzweil meets with Mulder again to give him more information.

see-through and feels like sticky gelatin. His internal organs—like his heart, liver, and kidneys—have been partially eaten away by the virus.

While Scully examines the body, Mulder meets with Kurtzweil again. The doctor warns Mulder that the syndicate is involved in a secret government "project" to deliberately release a terrible plague. He says the syndicate has been working on the project for over fifty years! But Kurtzweil can't or won't give Mulder any proof—he tells him to go to Dallas to search for the truth.

With this new information, Mulder asks Scully to meet him at the FBI field office in Dallas, Texas. There

of the model. It is hard to get it matched up just right in closeups and to make it look as if his feet are really touching the floor of the model. It is also difficult to match the lighting exactly, so that the light hitting the model matches the light hitting the actor. Watch old science-fiction movies closely. You will notice that the lighting on the giant spider, for example, doesn't match the lighting on the street he is walking down at all! That's because the spider was shot at a different time and in a different place than the street.

The movie climax takes place within the interior of a spaceship, settled beneath the ice in Antarctica.

The best solution was to build as much of the inside of the spaceship on stage as was possible. Those were the areas that Mulder would be seen walking on. In the background, the real set would be made to look much bigger with CG set extensions. Blue or green screens were hung all around the top of the real spaceship interior set. They were hung from pipes that were attached to the ceiling of the stage. This gave the visual effects artists a blue or green matte area into which they could add CG sets.

Those sets started as CG models. They were painted and textured to match the real set. Live-action footage from the real set—footage with David Duchovny in the hallways, for example—was scanned into the computer. The CG spaceship interior models were then added to the matte areas. The new composite shots were scanned back out to film.

Even though the movie finished shooting early in October, the visual effects team worked up until the following May. They continued shooting models and creating CG shots. Little by little, those effects shots were added to the movie. In May, the producers finally had a completed movie with spaceships, a huge spaceship interior, black worms, glaciers caving in, and exploding buildings!

All together, The X-Files movie required two and a half months of preparation and five months of filming. After it was all down on film it took another six months to complete the visual effects shots and edit the movie. Finally music and sound effects were added. The movie was completed at last. At the end of May 1998, thousands of copies of the movie were made. They went out to theaters all over the country for a June 1998 release.